Original title:
The Mossy Path

Copyright © 2025 Creative Arts Management OÜ
All rights reserved.

Author: Wyatt Kensington
ISBN HARDBACK: 978-1-80566-664-6
ISBN PAPERBACK: 978-1-80566-949-4

Nature's Carpet Unfurled

A carpet made of emerald fluff,
Where squirrels slide and rabbits puff.
The ferns do a little jig around,
While mushrooms wear hats, oh what a sound!

The leaves gossip like old friends,
Trading secrets, oh where it ends!
The daisies laugh with a silly twirl,
Nature's dance, give it a whirl!

A Sanctuary of Silent Green

In stillness, the ferns are plugged in,
While crickets play a violin.
Ol' Toad croaks a ballad in style,
With a nose for jazz, he croaks a while!

Here sits the snail, racing through time,
In a shell that jingles, it's quite sublime!
The ants hold a union meeting today,
Arguing who gets the biggest crumb buffet!

The Thrum of Life in Stillness

A beetle spins tales in the grass,
Telling bugs, "I'm first in class!"
Grasshoppers take a lunch break snack,
Chasing flies, oh what a hack!

The stillness hums a lively tune,
While butterflies dance beneath the moon.
The flowers pop popcorn, what a sight!
At this picnic, they all take flight!

Almost Akimbo in the Essence of Age

Old trees twist like grandpas in pain,
They joke about the weather's bane.
The bark is cracked like a laugh line,
Telling stories with every sign!

The wayward vines play hopscotch along,
Reciting verses of nature's song.
A wise old owl hoots with glee,
"Who's the funniest? It's definitely me!"

Treads of Time in Leafy Halls

In leafy halls where squirrels play,
I tripped on roots, oh what a day!
A turtle laughed, it took its time,
As I rolled past in my own rhyme.

The acorns dropped like tiny bombs,
I ducked and dodged, avoiding qualms.
A chipmunk waved, said "What a show!"
I winked and joined the silly flow.

Beneath the Dappled Sunlight

Beneath the trees where shadows dance,
   I tried to catch a sunlight glance.
A butterfly laughed, too quick for me,
   As I stumbled on a bumblebee.

The flowers giggled, dressed in bright,
   While I got lost, oh what a sight!
A ladybug took me on a ride,
Through petals wide and leaves that hide.

Shadows of the Overhanging Boughs

In shadows dark, I found my socks,
Hanging high amidst squawking mocks.
A crow cawed loud, gave me a scare,
As I danced 'round, searching everywhere.

The branches waved, just like my hands,
In a wacky jig where no one stands.
I thought I'd bring back quite the tale,
But tripped instead on a wiggly snail.

Lost in the Tangle of Green

In tangle thick, I lost my shoe,
A raccoon grinned, said, "Join my crew!"
We danced a jig on twigs and leaves,
As laughter floated through the eves.

A hedgehog snorted, rolled in glee,
As I pirouetted, feeling free.
But then I fell, oh what a sight,
In the embrace of green delight!

Petals and Pathways

On a stroll through blooms so bright,
I tripped on roots in pure delight.
Flowers giggle, petals sway,
As I tumble, they shout, "Hooray!"

Bees dance close, all in a spin,
I yield my snacks to buzz and grin.
With every step, a new surprise,
Nature laughs as I realize.

Where Ferns Whisper Secrets

Ferns share tales in rustling tones,
I swear they gossip more than phones.
With every rustle, secrets brew,
I nod along, pretending too.

A curious toad leaps by my shoe,
He winks at me, as if he knew.
I ponder if he's smart or sly,
Either way, he hops on by.

A Place for Solitude

With a grin, I seek my space,
But find a squirrel staring with grace.
He shields his stash; it's quite a sight,
But now I'm stuck sharing my bite.

I ponder if I should retreat,
Yet he twirls around, so light on feet.
I wonder if he's more alone,
Than I, with seeds and acorns shown.

Green Tapestry Awaits

The ferns and moss form a quilt,
Where butterflies weave like silk.
I take a seat, but lo and behold,
A snail claims it with dreams untold.

Around, the green begins to chat,
In muffled tones beneath my hat.
Who knew that nature had such flair?
A snail, a plant, and all that air!

The Forest's Gentle Embrace

In a forest where squirrels wear shoes,
And branches gossip about the day's news,
Fungi dance like they're in a ballet,
While a snail shouts, 'Hey, get out of my way!'

A tree tried to hug me, big and grand,
But its bark was rough, not like I'd planned,
I left with a laugh and a slight little bruise,
Next time I'll stick to the softest of views.

Steps on the Softened Stone

In the brook, the pebbles chime a tune,
As frogs croak out their afternoon croon,
I slip on a rock, send splashes around,
The fish all giggle, it's their fun playground!

A turtle races with all of its charm,
While I stumble, trying to avoid harm,
The slippery path calls to all of my fate,
Perhaps turtles were meant to go out on a date.

Echoes of Nature's Quiet Breath

The owls hold meetings high up in trees,
Discussing the habits of bumblebee teas,
A rabbit misheard, said, 'Let's have a feast!'
But all they did was laugh, at the worried beast!

The breeze carries whispers of jokes by the pond,
Where lily pads float, of which I've grown fond,
With each little ripple, they giggle with cheer,
I join in the laughter, it's what I hold dear.

Wandering in Verdure's Grasp

A lizard in sunglasses is basking in light,
While I tripped on a vine, gave quite the scare fright,
With a tumble and giggle, I rolled through the dew,
Next time I'll try walking in shoes that are blue!

Mushrooms peek out, saying 'Come take a look!',
But they're plotting to steal my favorite book,
'It's full of great pranks!' I can hear them devise,
As I chuckle at nature's amusing surprise.

Exploring the Veil of Growth

A squishy step on nature's floor,
Gives quite a giggle, oh what a chore!
The shoes get stuck, my foot takes flight,
I hop and skip, oh what a sight!

Green blankets hide secrets and bugs,
With each new squish, I share some shrugs.
A squirrel glances and cracks a grin,
As I tumble forward, laughing within.

Paths Woven with History

These trails are woven, threadbare and bold,
I trip on stories, rich yet untold.
At every twist, a chuckle erupts,
From missteps and dances, my pride interrupts.

Old roots sprawl out like old grandmas' tales,
I laugh with the trees and their musical gales.
With every stumble and every fall,
I'm weaving my antics into it all.

Stories Lurking in the Underbrush

Oh look, a shadow, what can it be?
A rabbit or ninja, can it be me?
Under the ferns, secrets do skitter,
In the wild world, life's a free hitter!

Whispers of laughter in rustling sets,
I keep my eye peeled for monstrous pets.
But all I find are glances and giggles,
As critters escape with their wiggly wiggles.

Sunbeams Through Mossy Altar

Sunbeams peek in, like giggling friends,
Illuminating chaos that never quite ends.
I pirouette through the dappled light,
Spotting a frog that's daring the height.

Each shimmer invites a silly dance,
While shadows cast doubt on my brave stance.
When nature winks, it's all just a game,
As I twirl through the sunlight (and feel a bit lame).

Twisted Roots and Gentle Breezes

Roots that tangle in silly knots,
They play games that tie up your thoughts.
The wind giggles through the leaves,
As squirrels plot what mischief they weave.

A chicken hatched with great surprise,
It danced in rhythm, oh what a guise!
Twirling 'round a bubbling brook,
Preening feathers like a storybook.

Secrets Among the Stones

Stones gossip about who's the boulder,
One claims it's him, just a bit older.
A pebble whispers with glee and pride,
Saying, "I've got quite a slick slide!"

Lichens chuckle, throwing shade,
While ants march in a parade.
Every crack has a tale to tell,
Of tumble and stumbles, oh quite well!

The Dance of Green and Gold

Leaves that twirl like they've lost their mind,
Chasing sunlight, they're so unconfined.
Golden rays shoot like silly darts,
While mossy carpets play their parts.

A caterpillar wiggled with flair,
Said, "One day, I'll fly through the air!"
But for now, he's as slow as a snail,
A green little dancer, on a leafy trail.

Where the Wild Things Whisper

In a clearing where shadows play peek,
Wild things gather for a cheeky sneak.
They share tall tales, each more absurd,
Of chasing rainbows and singing bird.

A raccoon in glasses reads a book,
While hedgehogs scamper and take a look.
"Is that a dance or just a fall?"
"Just hop and wiggle, we're having a ball!"

The Soft Pulse of Nature

In the woods, a squirrel sneezed,
Echoes ringing through the trees.
A rabbit laughed, quite unaware,
Of the pollen dancing in the air.

A turtle tripped, went for a slide,
On a leaf that took him for a ride.
The frogs all croaked a silly song,
While bees buzzed in, all day long.

The sun peeked through a playful gap,
Shining down on nature's map.
With every twist, with every turn,
New mischief waits, oh how we yearn!

So tread lightly, join the fun,
Here in shadows, laughter's spun.
Nature's pranks are quite the show,
Every step sparks joy, you know!

Footfalls on Timeless Ground

Each step I take, a crunching sound,
Like popcorn popping on the ground.
And every twig a hidden trap,
For sneaky critters, oh what a map!

A chipmunk dashed right past my shoe,
In glorious flight, like it always knew.
While ants held meetings, firm and proud,
Debating loudly, drawing a crowd.

A stick that looked just like a throne,
Invited me to sit and moan.
But wait! A beetle claimed it first,
Now who would win? The quest was burst!

Frogs jumped high, with silly grins,
As dragonflies cheered, waving their fins.
In this ground, where laughter's found,
Each footfall turns to joy unbound!

Revelations in the Muted Light

In dappled shade, a shadow pried,
A deer, surprised, jumped and skied.
While mushrooms giggled in delight,
As views emerged from fading light.

A raccoon wore a silly hat,
Declaring boldly, 'Ain't I fat?'
He stumbled perfectly on cue,
As if he knew just what to do.

The sunbeams winked, the breezes played,
Nature's jokes perfectly displayed.
As laughter danced along the trails,
Each whisper carried funny tales.

In this quiet, glowing drift,
Every moment's a perfect gift.
With jokes tucked in by nature's hand,
The secrets of light make laughter stand!

The Embrace of Entwined Roots

Underneath, where roots entwine,
A party's brewing, oh so fine.
With fuzzy socks and acorn hats,
The critters dance, there's no room for spats.

A raccoon juggling apples red,
While turtles dream of pies instead.
Chasing dreams on slippery trails,
Through laughter's echoes, joy prevails.

The wise old owl shared tales of yore,
But slumbering frogs just wanted more.
As grasshoppers brought out karaoke,
The singing flopped, oh what a hokey!

In tangled laughs, the roots conspire,
To create a mood that will inspire.
Here, beneath where laughter flows,
Entwined roots giggle, as friendship grows!

Ferns and Memory

Underfoot, the green blades dance,
They tickle toes, they make you prance.
In laughter shared, we trip and sway,
As shadows chuckle through the day.

Forgotten snacks from picnics past,
A sandwich lost—no need for fast!
We find old crumbs where nature hides,
And giggle loud as time abides.

A snail goes by, all in a rush,
We wave goodbye with no big hush.
He's on a quest, but what's the plan?
To find his way to Snail-O-Rama land!

In every step, sweet tales unfold,
With rustling ferns, and stories told.
We skip along, with silly glee,
Embracing every memory!

Beneath the Old Oak's Gaze

Beneath the branches, wide and stout,
A game of hide-and-seek—no doubt!
We giggle low, we sneak and peek,
What's that noise? A squirrel's cheek!

With acorns flying left and right,
It's a nutty war, oh, what a sight!
The laughter rolls like windblown leaves,
As we devise more cheeky thieves.

A bird sings loud, off-key and bright,
Is it a song or quite a fright?
We join along with our own tune,
A cacophony that makes hearts swoon.

Time drifts slow beneath this tree,
Where laughter roots down wild and free.
Each gaze meets joy, no need to chase,
Life's simple pleasures glow and grace!

Tracing the Earth's Gentle Spine

We wander down the winding trail,
With silly shoes that squeak and grail.
A puddle laughs, we leap and splash,
Our giggles ring out, a joyous bash.

The pebbles roll like tumbleweed,
They tickle toes, light-hearted deed.
We march in line, a silly crew,
As ants parade with plans anew.

A feisty rabbit, quick and sly,
Darts past us with a playful cry.
"Catch me if you can!" it seems to say,
We chase it down, then lose our way!

Each twist and turn brings joy anew,
While trees tell tales that feel so true.
In every step, a laugh unwinds,
The Earth beneath our feet, so kind!

Where Wildflowers Bloom

Wildflowers pop, a vibrant sight,
In hues so bold, they spark delight.
We take a stroll through colors bright,
With bees that buzz, and smells just right.

A daisy winks, a silly pose,
It sways and dances as the wind blows.
We join the show, a goofy twist,
Each flower grins, none can resist.

Butterflies flit with mischief in mind,
They flitter off, 'Come catch me,' they bind!
We stumble, giggle, fall in dismay,
Nature's jesters, come out to play!

With petals soft, we weave our crowns,
As laughter echoes all around.
A riot of colors, a great delight,
In wildflower fields, the world feels right!

Whispers in the Underbrush

A squirrel's chatter fills the air,
While rabbits hide without a care.
With acorns rolling, such a mess,
Nature's jesters, I confess.

The leaves do dance, they play their game,
As if the trees are calling names.
Two frogs leap high with comic flair,
One lands in puddles—splashing everywhere!

A snail decides to race a bug,
But takes a nap—oh, what a shrug!
The ants just laugh and scurry fast,
While knowing who will finish last.

Yet as I stroll with joy and cheer,
Nature's humor brings us near.
With every laugh, I hear the call,
Of woodland friends, I've met them all.

Secrets of the Forgotten Trail

Vines are tangled, roots out of place,
Whispers linger with a cheeky grace.
A deer trips over a hidden stone,
Then shakes his head, just like a drone.

The path is crooked, full of twists,
With hidden laughs that nature insists.
A mouse in boots slips down a hill,
While crickets chuckle at their thrill.

A stoic owl gives quizzical looks,
As I explore through ancient books.
But page by page, it seems he's lost,
No wisdom here, just laughs at cost.

Beneath the trees, I roam and play,
Finding joy in silly ways.
For secrets dwell where laughter grows,
On paths that only nature knows.

Nature's Green Tapestry

In threads of green, the world is spun,
A patchwork quilt of joy and fun.
With daisies laughing in the breeze,
And playful shadows from the trees.

The brook is gurgling jokes anew,
As sunbeams dance with morning dew.
A ladybug rolls 'round on a leaf,
While gossiping with a nearby chief.

The flowers tap their petals light,
In every color, bold and bright.
The butterflies, in fancy dress,
Twirl about and make a mess.

Through every crack and every glen,
Nature's humor draws me in.
Abundant joy with every glance,
In this green world, we all can dance.

Shadows Beneath the Canopy

Beneath the boughs where shadows creep,
A raccoon naps, in dreams so deep.
The whispers of the leaves are sly,
As squirrels plot their next supply.

The beams of light tease lizards bold,
As sunlit stories unfold.
But watch your step, a twig may crack,
And lead to giggles on your back!

A fox in shades tries to blend in,
But his fluffy tail gives him a spin.
With every rustle, chaos reigns,
As creatures jest with merry gains.

Yet while I wander, dappled and free,
Nature's comedy stretches to me.
In hidden corners where critters await,
Each shadow holds a funny fate.

Glimmers of Forgotten Lore

In the woods where gnomes do play,
A squirrel steals a snack each day.
With a wink and a twitch of paws,
He claims it's his because of laws.

But they say he's just a furry thief,
With no regard for the greenleaf chief.
He scampers and hides with all his might,
Yet leaves crumbs in the soft moonlight.

Whispers float like dandelion puffs,
As creatures share their secret gruffs.
"Did you see that!" one critter squeaks,
"Danced like a fool on two left weeks!"

Amid the giggles of the night's delight,
The trees shake with laughter, what a sight!
For every twig and leaf that sways,
A story emerges, in humorous ways.

Enchantment Beside the Bark

By the old oak, a fox prances,
In his shiny coat, he takes his chances.
With a flick of his tail, he starts a game,
Calling all critters, to join his fame.

The badger yawns, says, "Not tonight!"
While the rabbit is busy with carrot bites.
Yet the owl, wise with a twinkling eye,
Conjures up jokes that make spirits fly.

"Why did the beetle wear a crown?"
The laughter echoes all around.
"Because he ruled the roly-poly balls,
Though he trips on grass and stumbles and falls!"

In the giggles and chuckles that drift through the wood,
Every creature feels understood.
With a hop, a skip, and a spring in their heart,
The night's enchantment is a comical art.

The Lullaby of the Leafy Realm

In the leafy realm where shadows dance,
A mushroom sings to a firefly prance.
"Come join the show, oh creatures small,
Let's have a ball by the old stone wall!"

The hedgehog shimmies, a sight to behold,
While the worms do twist, so brave and bold.
But a tumble and roll sends them all in a spin,
"Don't worry!" cries the hedgehog, "Let's start again!"

A raccoon juggles acorns with flair,
While giggling weasels hang in midair.
"Who knew leaves could be so spry?"
As the moonlight winks from way up high.

Under the stars, with a wink and a cheer,
Every laugh echoes far and near.
In the lullaby of nature's bright gleam,
Where jokes are spun like an enchanted dream.

Foliage's Gentle Invitation

Beneath the boughs, the crickets play,
Crafting a symphony for another day.
"Mosey on over!" a tiny voice calls,
"Join the grand feast, we've lots of balls!"

The grasshopper, proud, boasts of his hop,
While the ant insists, "I'll never stop!"
With a little bit of dance and a lot of zest,
The woodland creatures prepare for the fest.

The thistle sways with a giggle and grace,
As the lark shares tales, oh what a place!
"Did you hear about the rumor, quite absurd?
That no one believes in the flying bird?"

Joy alarms ring as laughter is spun,
In foliage's embrace, the fun's just begun.
Every leaf joins in with a playful sway,
As night turns the path to a grand ballet.

The Undergrowth's Serenade

In tangled greens, I trip and slide,
A dance with roots, oh what a ride!
Frogs croak tunes, they call my name,
As I waltz with them, it's all a game.

The bushes giggle, the trees all sway,
They whisper secrets in the light of day.
I'm lost in laughter, with every step,
Who knew wild paths could be such a prep?

A squirrel shimmies, joins my prance,
He gives a nod; it's our wild dance.
Nature's concert, a quirky sight,
In the undergrowth, I'm full of delight.

With every stumble, I smile and cheer,
This silly adventure brings me near.
To creatures who chuckle, and welcome me,
On this winding journey, I'm wildly free.

Echoing Footsteps on Old Trails

Through leaves and twigs, I tread so bold,
The echoes laugh, stories unfold.
Each footstep sings, a bouncy tune,
As if the path says, 'Join my swoon!'

I shuffle past a twisty vine,
It tickles my legs, oh how divine!
With every turn and jolly bounce,
I feel the forest laugh and pounce.

A bear peeks out, surprised to see,
A clumsy chap like a bumblebee.
He shakes his head, and gives a grin,
And round we go, with a cheeky spin.

Rippling chuckles fill the air,
As I trip over roots without a care.
The woodland chorus raises cheer,
On old trails here, there's nothing to fear!

Moss-Covered Memories

On ancient stones, the green hugs tight,
Each step I take is a funny fright.
A slip and slide on this soft, thick bed,
I laugh so hard, my face turns red.

The mossy carpet knows my name,
It whispers jokes, it's all a game.
Each squishy patch, a friendly nod,
As I bounce along, feeling quite odd.

Old logs giggle as I pass by,
With snickers hidden from the sky.
The memories cling like dew on grass,
Stumbling forward, let the good times last!

Nature's playground, wild and free,
With every blunder, it's just me.
On these mossy tales, I stand tall,
Laughing through life, I'll never fall!

Beneath the Quiet Canopy

In shady nooks where shadows play,
I try to sneak, but trip away.
The leaves all giggle, the branches sway,
As I juggle snacks on my funny fray.

A squirrel remarks, with paws on his chest,
'Your clumsy style is simply the best!'
I offer him chips; he frowns with grace,
But then does a dance, oh what a case!

Beneath the boughs, laughter sprouts,
As I trip, tumble and roll about.
The sun peeks in with a mischievous grin,
Cheering me on as I twist and spin.

With every hop, I shed a care,
In this forest bonanza, I gladly share.
So here's to the fun, the stumbles, the glee,
Under this canopy, I'm wild and free!

Veils of Green and Gold

A slippery slope, a great big laugh,
Frogs jump high, they take a half.
With every step, a squishy sound,
Apologies, dear shoes, it's muddy ground.

Laughter echoes beneath the trees,
Nature dances with the breeze.
Worms wiggle in a fancy show,
Oh, the fun that they bestow!

Every twist, a surprise delight,
A squirrel steals my snack in flight.
Nature's antics, oh so grand,
Who knew a stroll could be so planned?

With every turn, a giggle or two,
Sometimes I swear the trees laugh too!
In this jungle of glee, we stand tall,
With the green and gold, we have it all.

A Passageway to Stillness

On this carefree trail, we jog and shout,
With every step, we dance about.
A misplaced shoe, an errant heel,
Oh, the splinters—what a deal!

Squirrels mock us from above,
Chasing tails, a game of love.
Stumbling over twigs like pros,
I think my balance really blows.

A hermit crab pots on the way,
Here, there, and gone in a fray.
Underneath the shade of trees,
Even the bumblebees tease with ease!

With giggles bright, we dash and twirl,
Nature's playground makes us whirl.
In this stillness, we find our cheer,
Who knew hiking could spread such zing?

In Nature's Cradle

In a cradle of green, we skip and run,
Dodging bugs, it's all in fun.
A nesting bird gives us a glare,
"Keep it down! Here's our lair!"

Wobbling mushrooms wave hello,
As we pass, their fanciful show.
A butterfly flits, says, "Join this game!"
"Oh, we will! But I want a name!"

The grass tickles as we tumble down,
Rolling like clowns, minus the frown.
We laugh so hard, the trees do sway,
Who knew nature could brighten the day?

With laughter ringing, our spirits soar,
We find new paths, then find some more.
In this cradle, we lay our stakes,
Nature giggles as we make our breaks.

Murmurs of the Underbrush

Whispers dance in the shaded glade,
Critters gossip in their parade.
A chipmunk grins, it's yours to guess,
While I just trip in my own mess!

A rustle here, a shuffle there,
Nature plays its prank with flair.
An ant parade, oh what a sight,
I think they're picking a food fight!

Beneath the leaves, the laughter echos,
Wisdom hides while chaos grows.
Who knew bushes could have such cheer?
A comedy show, it's all right here!

Every step, a quirky find,
In the underbrush, we unwind.
With joy and laughter, we take flight,
In this quirky world, all feels right.

A Drift Through Thickets

I wandered into brush with glee,
Laughter lost in every tree.
A squirrel chattered, quite absurd,
As if it said, 'Halt, word nerd!'

Rustling leaves kept mocking me,
'You're late for tea, can't you see?'
But I'd rather joke with roots,
Than sip with snobs in fancy boots.

Branches wave as if to dance,
I twirl and spin in my own chance.
Bumbles buzz with silly sounds,
Making fun of my tight bounds.

With every step, a giggle blooms,
Nature's fun, like playful cartoons.
Through thickets thick, I drift away,
In this wild, whimsical ballet.

Footsteps in the Forgetfulness

I trod along a path unsure,
With pebbles that just want to lure.
Each step a chuckle, slip, then flop,
As clumsy worms my shoes do swap.

Oh, leaves above were laughing loud,
I joined the antics, felt so proud.
A superhero with mud-stained pants,
In this aerial vine-filled dance.

A badger shrugged, 'You've options, mate!
Why fret about a silly fate?'
I winked at him, then tripped again,
A comedy sketch turned zen.

So here I am, a merry mess,
With puzzled trees, my game of chess.
Wandering deep in blissful daze,
Each footfall a new laugh to praise.

The Journey in Leafy Labyrinths

I ventured forth, oh what a maze!
With leafy walls that twist and gaze.
A rabbit yelled, 'Wrong way, my friend!'
Which only made the fun extend.

Through vines and twigs, I made a vow,
'I'll find my way, I'll show them how!'
Yet each turn led me right back here,
To giggle fits and absent cheer.

A wise old owl gave me a wink,
'Find humor first, then stop to think.'
So I danced with shadows, made my claim,
In this leafy world, I lost my name.

Pathless forests can sure confuse,
But laughter's the path we always choose.
In this tangled grip of fun and jest,
The journey's a game, and I'm its best!

Nature's Hidden Mosaic

In patches green, a puzzle lies,
With hues of laughter in disguise.
A butterfly whispered, 'Come and play!'
'But first, watch out for the gumdrop sway!'

Footsteps fumbled on candy grass,
While daisies giggled, preparing to sass.
Each bloom a character, bright and bold,
Their jokes unfold like tales retold.

I joined a parade of wobbly ants,
Who make great efforts for tiny plants.
They chuckled, 'Stay, this game is grand!'
And lo and behold, their joke reprimand.

In nature's art, I made my stance,
Chasing whims in a merry dance.
For every misstep, a jest did grow,
In this hidden world, I'm part of the show!

A Journey Through Verdant Veils

In the woods where the critters play,
I lost my way on a bright green day.
Slipped on a leaf and tumbled down,
Laughed by a squirrel in a fuzzy crown.

Every turn leads to a curious sight,
A tree wearing socks, what a funny sight!
The mushrooms chuckle, the breeze gives a tease,
As I dance with a hedgehog, both feeling at ease.

Lichen-Laden Footsteps

Walking slow where the moss is thick,
My shoes just pulled a funny trick.
They stuck to a patch, quite sly and stout,
And now I'm the one who's standing out!

Wiggle and jiggle, don't trip on a toad,
A worm tells a joke—such a silly road!
With laughter surrounding as I skip and hop,
I wave to the mushrooms, my wobbly stop!

Echoes of the Forest Floor

In the forest where shadows toss,
I'm talking to twigs, oh what a loss!
They whisper secrets, I nod and grin,
A chat with the roots, where humor begins.

A fox wearing glasses reads a tall tale,
While snails race each other, oh what a trail!
With every crunch of leaves beneath,
Nature's a comedian, so refreshingly brief.

The Hidden Trail's Embrace

Now wandering where the brambles lean,
Found a rabbit in overalls, quite the scene!
He taught me to dance with an acorn hat,
While humming along with a friendly bat.

The ferns wave hello, a tickling breeze,
I trip on a gnome who's resting with ease.
In this quirky place of laughter and cheer,
I'm lost for a while, but it's perfectly clear.

A Journey Through Verdant Shadows

Beneath the trees, I trip and fall,
A squirrel laughs, oh, how they call!
I scurry up, my pride is torn,
These woodland friends, so well adorned.

With mossy shoes, I tread with glee,
A toadstool party waits for me.
They dance and sing, so bold and spry,
In hidden realms where mischief flies.

The grass bows low, as if to tease,
While fairies chuckle, on the breeze.
I wave hello, they wink and cheer,
This leafy path is full of cheer!

A frog recites a quirky rhyme,
As I lose track of space and time.
With each odd turn, another laugh,
In nature's joy, I've found my path.

Trails of Green Enchantment

A leafy lane where whispers hide,
A bunny leaps, I step aside.
He gives a wink, oh what a sight,
In this green realm, all feels just right.

A crooked stick, my trusted guide,
Leads to where the wild things bide.
A gnome with shades gives me a grin,
Come join the fun, let's all jump in!

A bear in slippers, what a craze!
He leads a dance with woodland praise.
With every twirl, my worries fade,
In this green world, I'm not afraid.

As wildflowers bloom, I giggle loud,
In this embrace, I feel so proud.
With nature's crew, the world seems bright,
On paths of green, my heart takes flight!

Embrace of Earth and Sky

With every step, a thud, a bounce,
The world around me starts to pounce.
A worm with style wiggles by,
In this embrace, I just can't lie.

A tangled web, a spider's dome,
Invites me in, feels like a home.
Witty banter from butterflies,
In twirls and flutters, they improvise.

The wind, it tickles as I stride,
I laugh aloud, can't run or hide.
Oh mighty oak, you sway and sway,
In this bright realm, I long to stay.

A squirrel juggles acorns—oh dear!
The laughter echoes, spread good cheer.
I dance along, lost in the play,
In this embrace, forever stay!

Secret Groves in Twilight

In twilight's grasp, the shadows twine,
A critter choir sings, so divine.
With chuckles soft and eyes aglow,
These secret groves put on a show.

A raccoon wearing a tiny hat,
Invites me in, like, "How 'bout that?"
His gang of friends all start to prance,
And under stars, we join the dance.

The moon plays tricks, a shining light,
On rabbits leaping with delight.
In whispered tales of charm and fun,
The night is young; the party's begun!

With fireflies flashing like disco balls,
We bop and weave 'til nature calls.
In secret groves, I've found my place,
In nightly mischief, my heart has space.

The Silence That Speaks

In shadows deep where whispers dwell,
A squirrel talks, but who can tell?
With acorn hats, they prance around,
Their giggles echo, lost and found.

The trees nod back with leafy grins,
While mushrooms sport their little sins.
The groundhog's dance, a wobbly show,
Three cheers for dirt, they steal the show!

A snail races slow in a leafy race,
"Catch me!" it shouts, with slime on its face.
The moon takes notes, in quirky light,
As critters play till the end of night.

So if you listen, you might just hear,
The chatter of creatures, far and near.
For laughter lurks in hidden nooks,
In nature's silence, the joy still cooks.

Secrets Carried in Soft Footfalls

On padded paws, they sneak and spy,
A froggy band with dreams to fly.
Their secret meetings, by the creek,
With croaks and croons, the fun they seek.

The rabbits hop with tricks to share,
While hedgehogs roll without a care.
"Let's tell a joke!" the wise owl hoots,
And mischief brews in furry suits.

A chatty mouse with cheese in tow,
Plays hide and seek, but what a show!
"Touch my tail and I'll squeak loud!"
A giggle from the leafy crowd.

Each tiny footfall sings a song,
Of tales and laughter, where they belong.
In nature's court, their secrets blend,
In soft footfalls, the joy won't end.

Enchanted by Nature's Breath

A buzzing bee with dreams of gold,
Tripped on a petal, quite uncontrolled.
It whirled around, a dizzy dance,
Declared itself the king of chance.

The flowers laughed, a riot of hues,
As butterflies donned their fancy shoes.
A caterpillar struts with flair,
Wiggling as if it didn't care.

The sun peeked in, with gleamy smile,
While squirrels plotted a cheeky style.
"Let's throw a party, it's time to play!"
And nature giggled, come what may.

With silly sounds and vibrant sights,
Each critter joins the wild delights.
In laughter's grasp, they sing and sway,
Enchanted moments, bright as day.

Where Memories Meet Moss

On velvet greens, the mischief spawns,
With mushrooms wearing silly fawns.
A raccoon plays a tambourine,
To serenade the forest scene.

Old logs murmur tales of the past,
Of raccoons, skunks, and shadows cast.
They chuckle soft, in whispered tones,
As laughter spills from mossy stones.

A dapper toad, with bowtie neat,
Instructs the ants on how to greet.
With tiny hats, they waltz around,
A grand parade, in joy unbound.

So tread with care on emerald beds,
Where laughter blooms and humor spreads.
In every nook, a giggle waits,
Where memories dance, and fun elates.

Curves in the Emerald Hue

Beneath the trees, I weave and sway,
A slip here and there, oh what a play!
A frog jumps high, gives me a fright,
Who knew moss could bounce with such delight?

I trip on roots, a comedic dance,
Nature's gym, I'm in a trance.
A squirrel watches with a chuckle and cheer,
While I'm dodging spores, look out, my dear!

A snail cruises by, oh so sleek,
"Slow and steady," he says, "is my peak!"
Yet here I tumble, like a clumsy fool,
Winning gold inside my own silly duel.

Now laughter echoes in emerald hues,
Life's little blunders, I'm free to choose.
With every step, a joyfully slip,
I dance with the whims, let my troubles flip.

Lanterns of Dew and Dawn

Morning breaks with dew drops bright,
I slip on grass, oh what a sight!
A ladybug lands on my nose just right,
I sneeze so loud, it takes off in flight!

Sunlight glimmers, a sparkling show,
I slip on a puddle, down I go!
My laughter mingles with birds in the sky,
As a worm waves hello, oh my, oh my!

Each step a giggle, each stumble a cheer,
Nature's comedy is crystal clear.
In this morning frolic, I'm light as a fawn,
Dewy adventures greet each new dawn.

With droplets like lanterns, they twinkle and shine,
Each giggle and chuckle, a well-timed rhyme.
My path may be slippery, but I'm not dismayed,
In the dance of the morn, my spirit's unfrayed.

Whispers Beneath the Canopy

Beneath the branches, whispers hum,
A humorous breeze, oh where you come?
I wander lost, my map's in my head,
Chasing squirrels, pretending I'm fed!

Footsteps echo on soft, squishy ground,
While giggles from grasshoppers flit all around.
A mushroom laughs as I ponder and frown,
"Just one more step, don't let me down!"

Clothes covered in dirt, a fabulous sight,
I wear them with pride, I'm a mess, what's right?
An owl gives me side-eye, quite unimpressed,
While I juggle acorns and strive to impress.

Laughter and whispers beneath leafy trees,
Nature joins in with a whimsical tease.
In this silly forest, come join the game,
Each bump and each tumble a badge without shame.

Lichen Dreams

In a land where lichen sprout and thrive,
I chase my dreams, feeling so alive.
But oh dear, what a tangled affair,
As my foot gets caught in a mossy snare!

A beetle plays peek-a-boo with glee,
"Careful now, don't trip over me!"
I laugh with delight, my face in a grin,
As I tumble again and the fun begins!

With every step, a new giggle unfolds,
The forest is quirky with stories untold.
A lichen with wisdom, a sage of the scene,
"Life's a wild ride, keep it light and keen!"

So here in the green, let antics abound,
With laughter and joy, I stumble around.
In dreams made of lichen, I find my true cue,
To embrace all the giggles, so fresh and so new.

Roots that Bind the Lost

In the forest deep, where squirrels play,
Roots like octopuses twist and sway.
They grab my shoes as I try to flee,
I laugh so hard, I tumble with glee.

A bird up high gives me a wink,
As I ponder life and how to think.
These roots, they tease, they pull and pry,
Making me wonder if I can fly.

The trees all chuckle, their branches bent,
At my clumsy dance—was it really meant?
With every step, the earth's a prank,
"Oh dear!" I shout, "It's a rooty tank!"

So if you wander with a merry heart,
Watch those roots! They'll play their part.
Embrace the silliness, let it stick,
Because in this forest, life's a comic trick.

Dance of the Woodland Spirits

In the twilight glow, they take a leap,
Woodland spirits with mischievous peep.
They twirl around on a sylvan stage,
Making me giggle, acting their age.

With acorns tossed and leaves in flight,
They shout and squeal in delight at night.
"Catch me if you can!" they playfully cry,
But oh! I'm not spry, I can only sigh.

A frog joins in, giving it a whirl,
Chasing fireflies, it gives a twirl.
I stumble forth, feeling quite slick,
Only to trip on a glowing stick.

Laughter echoes through the leafy sea,
As I flail and flop, just like a bee.
In this magical dance, I find my groove,
In the woodland light, I'm ready to move.

Curves of Nature's Exquisite Art

Nature's curves in splendid grace,
Create a maze where I've lost face.
Twirling around, my feet get caught,
In playful shapes that life has wrought.

Each bend and twist, a giggle starts,
As I navigate this maze of arts.
With every turn, I stumble anew,
"Why is this so curvy? Who made this zoo?"

The trees all arch, like laughing friends,
While I wobble on, where the trail bends.
And just when I think I've hit a knack,
A root jumps out! Oh, the floors attack!

So as I wander, lost yet free,
I embrace the art of hilarity.
For in each curve, a chuckle rings,
In nature's dance, the joy it brings.

Softness Underfoot

A carpet of green, it cushions my fall,
With every step, I'm having a ball.
Mushrooms pop up with a grin so wide,
"Come on, dear friend, let's go for a ride!"

My shoes get stuck in a squishy thrill,
While puddles laugh, giving me a chill.
"Hey! Watch your step!" the mossy ground teases,
As I bounce and giggle while nature pleases.

A badger peeks from behind a tree,
With a sly little chuckle, it winks at me.
Sliding and slipping, it joins the spree,
In this plush wonderland, we dance with glee.

So if you tread softly on this lush bed,
Be ready for laughter—just follow your head.
For underfoot softness invites such fun,
In this playful world, the joy has begun.

Lost in Nature's Caress

I slipped on a shoe, it flew through the air,
Landed on a squirrel, who gave me a stare.
Dancing with daisies, I tripped on a vine,
Whispering secrets, the trees drank my wine.

A frog in a top hat, with laughter so loud,
Said, "Join my parade! You should be so proud!"
With branches as banners, we twirled and we spun,
Nature's shy beauty, having far too much fun.

The sun hid its face, but the clouds wore a grin,
As I joined with the daisies, a tangle I'm in.
Bees buzzing softly, a cheerful brigade,
Conducting the orchestra of joy that we made.

Yet onward I wandered, lost in this bliss,
Tripping on whispers, I felt nature's kiss.
A tumble, a giggle, I'm covered in leaves,
I'll paint the whole forest with these silly eves.

Dreams of Dappled Light

Beneath a great oak, my feet went for strolls,
I waltzed through the shadows, avoiding the trolls.
But trolls are just fairies in disguise, you'll behold,
With odd jiggly laughs that are sweetly retold.

I saw dancing mushrooms, with smiles so spry,
Then a snail gave a wink, oh my! How time flies!
They offered me tea, in a thimble so small,
With biscuits that giggled, and a punch line for all.

The sun dripped like honey through branches above,
It tickled my senses with rays full of love.
I juggled with acorns, they bounced off my nose,
As the wind whispered secrets, in breezy repose.

With each silly slip, I embraced nature's song,
A tango with twigs, feeling ever so strong.
In this patch of delight, I frolicked with glee,
Lost in the warmth where I yearned to be.

A Tread on Ancient Ground

With each step I take, the earth gives a cheer,
Crickets all chuckle, saying, "She's here!"
I dance on the roots, intertwined like a braid,
While a mischievous pebble plots tricks to invade.

A rabbit in glasses reads poetry loud,
He argues with worms who boast, "We're quite proud!"
Together they giggle, the ground starts to spin,
As butterflies join in, creating a din.

I trespass through memories, the old trees now sigh,
With limbs that are tangled, they reach for the sky.
An ancient oak chuckles, "You're better than bread,
With your giggles and wiggles, you lighten our dread!"

So here on this ground, where history's spun,
I wiggle my toes and twirl just for fun.
With laughter for soil and joy as the seed,
I'll plant my adventures where silliness leads.

The Crawler's Soft Serenade

A caterpillar crooned as he sashayed along,
With silken soft notes, he was singing a song.
The ants joined the chorus, a tap-dancing crew,
While fluttering buddies made musical dew.

They twirled under leaves, in the cool shaded haze,
Creating a ruckus in nature's vast maze.
With beats from the beetles, my heart skipped a beat,
While ladybugs giggled at their own tiny feet.

"Oh, wiggle and giggle!" the garden exclaimed,
Each crawl a new rhythm; nothing was tamed.
The sun painted smiles on each critter's face,
As I snickered with glee at this fanciful space.

When evening approached, I waved them goodbye,
With dreams in my pocket and twinkling eyes.
The night would bring the stars, their dance would ignite,
While the crawler's soft serenade whispered delight.

Murmurs of the Wandering Stream

A gurgle giggles through the trees,
As water tickles roots with ease.
The frogs engage in a singing spree,
While fish joke 'bout their swimming spree.

With splashes bright, they spin and flail,
Each wave a tale, a twisting trail.
The dragonflies dance with comic flair,
While turtles grin, they just don't care.

Beneath the Canopy's Silence

Squirrels plot in secretive huddles,
Do they squeak of nuts or colorful puddles?
An acorn flies, a split-second fling,
Oh dear, it's all part of their spring fling!

The leaves chuckle as they sway,
Which critter will trip on a random buffet?
Laughter echoes through boughs so spry,
With merry mischief, the creatures just fly.

The Texture of Time in Green

Fungi fashion hats for the most trendy,
While snails race to be the friendliest.
Every step on leaf is a clumsy sound,
Socks and sandals make fashion astound!

The breeze brushes through, tickles the ground,
A tumbleweed giggles, round and round.
Grasses nod, they don't want to fight,
As worms disco dance under low light.

In the Realm of Shadows and Light

Sunbeams wink at the shadows bold,
Do they tell tales or secrets untold?
Bats play tag with whispers of night,
Laughing hard, causing quite the fright!

Each flicker and skip, a light-hearted tease,
While owls roll their eyes at the giggling breeze.
A creature pops up just for the fun,
Shouting, 'I swear, I'm the cleverest one!'

Breath of the Old Woods

In a forest where critters play,
The squirrels dart, oh what a display!
With acorns flying like tiny bombs,
Who knew trees could have such charms?

A wise old owl, perched with grace,
Winks at me with a feathery face.
"Hoot your delight, join in the fun,
Dance with shadows, while we outrun!"

Underneath a mushroom's cap,
A gnome snoozes, what a nap!
He dreams of dances, of skipping stones,
Still, he snores like a bear in tones!

With sunbeams flickering, shadows fall,
I've tripped and stumbled, but oh, what a ball!
In this laughter-filled wood, I'm free,
With twigs for crowns—come, dance with me!

Serpentine Paths of Pine

Along the creek, the pathway twists,
Each turn reveals a new surprise—oh, the trysts!
A rabbit hops, and jumps too high,
"You'll ruin your dinner!" I laugh, oh my!

Beneath the boughs, a bear takes a seat,
Enjoying honey, oh what a treat!
He grumbles softly, 'It's all mine, you see!
But if you share, I'll dance for thee!'

The gusty wind sings a cheeky tune,
As squirrels compete in a nutty swoon.
In this maze of laughter, I can't help but see,
Paths of pine lead to fun and glee!

A log rolls by, quite the prankster,
With a pull of my sock—what a dank jester!
In the woods, all is quirky and bright,
With nature's comedy, pure delight!

Amongst the Ferns and Flax

In the shade where ferns like to sway,
A chicken hops, trying to play!
"Why did you cross?" I jokingly crow,
"To get to the other side—don't you know?"

A quirky moose struts with pride,
Winking at me with eyes open wide.
Wearing a hat made of leaves and twine,
He bows with style, oh isn't he fine?

The flax blooms in colors, quite bold,
A snail races, or so I've been told.
"Wait for me!" he shouts with a sigh,
"I thought you'd slow down; guess I'll just cry!"

Amongst the flora, laughter takes flight,
With silly antics, a comical sight.
In this green wonder, I giggle and dance,
Nature's own stage, a charming romance!

The Lure of Leafy Depths

In green corridors, where shadows tease,
A cat sneaks softly, with the greatest of ease.
But a twig snaps—oh what a fright!
She jumps ten feet, oh, what a sight!

Where the leaves whisper secrets profound,
A raccoon prances, scurries around.
"Why so serious?" he quips with a grin,
"Life is a game! Let the frolicking begin!"

The air is sweet with a tang of the wild,
While I trip over roots, like a clumsy child.
Upon a rock, a lizard sunbathes,
"Mornin', my friend, join my sunlit craze!"

In leafy depths, with laughter and cheer,
Every twist in the trail brings something near.
Wandering brightly, I chuckle and sway,
Finding pure joy in this whimsical play!

The Sway of Verdant Canopies

In a forest where squirrels play,
A frog jumps high, hip-hip-hooray!
The trees do a dance, oh what a sight,
As leaves whisper secrets late at night.

The grass is a trampoline, bouncy and bright,
The toads wear top hats, oh what a delight!
While birds sing off-key, it's quite a show,
In silly little hats, they steal the glow.

The sun peeks in, it's playing tag,
While chipmunks boast of their daily brag.
Every step's a giggle, every turn a jest,
In this wacky wild play, we're surely blessed.

So come take a stroll, let your laughter ring,
In a world where the odd is the key to spring.
Let the nature's cheer be our joyful tune,
As we skip along, 'neath a winking moon.

Where Light and Shadow Dance

In a glade where shadows tell a joke,
Sunlight winks as the branches poke.
The flowers are giggling, quite a scene,
As butterflies prance, all spry and keen.

A rabbit hops in a too-big shoe,
Says, 'Fashion's tough when you're furred like a stew!'
The sunbeams chuckle, hiding in the leaves,
While a plucky little ant does cartwheel thieves.

The shadows compete, make silly faces,
As squirrels perform in their acrobatic races.
Each light spark dances with a hint of tease,
While the breeze joins in, a tickling breeze.

So laugh into the dark, let joy be your guide,
Where whimsy and wonder are side by side.
Lose track of time, let your heart prance,
In this playful realm where shadows dance.

The Hidden Path of Tranquility

On a trail where laughter lightly roams,
A raccoon wears shades and calls it his home.
He dives in the snacks, oh what a feast,
As his pals laugh out loud, their fun never ceased.

The trees play peek-a-boo, so sprightly and spry,
With branches like arms that reach for the sky.
A hedgehog with glasses reads a sweet tale,
While sunbeams create a cozy, warm veil.

In nature's embrace, silliness reigns,
As butterflies giggle and the grass complains.
Here, peace wears a hat, as odd as can be,
And joy climbs high on the tallest tree.

So wander this route, let your smile grow,
In a land full of jest where the silly winds blow.
With every soft step, let your heart sing,
On this delightful journey where laughter takes wing.

Beneath the Canopy of Dreams

In a realm where the weird and the wacky align,
A snail wears a cape, and oh, how he shines!
He speeds with a swagger, almost like a champ,
While a party of fireflies plan the next stamp.

A whimsical owl with glasses so thick,
Hoots laughter at thoughts, oh man, what a trick!
The stars join the jam, throwing sparkles around,
As mushrooms spread gossip, so joyful, profound.

The breeze joins the dance, swaying with ease,
While squirrels host tea with acorns and cheese.
They toast to the magic, to fun in the trees,
In a spot where nonsense flows gently like seas.

So venture beneath where the dreams softly gleam,
Let your heart race wildly, laugh loud, and beam.
In this silly old world, let your worries drift,
For laughter's the treasure, the ultimate gift.

www.ingramcontent.com/pod-product-compliance
Lightning Source LLC
Chambersburg PA
CBHW071846160426
43209CB00003B/429